A Table Before Me

John W. Rilling

DAILY DEVOTIONS FROM LUKE'S GOSPEL

FORTRESS PRESS   PHILADELPHIA

CONTENTS

Biblical quotations from the Revised Standard Version of the Bible, copyrighted 1946, 1952, © 1971, 1973 by the Division of Christian Education of the National Council of the Churches of Christ in the U.S.A., are used by permission.

Library of Congress Catalog Card Number 76–007859
ISBN 0–8006–1230–2
5764J76   Printed in U.S.A.   1–1230

INTRODUCTION

Well known is the judgment of Ernest Renan, the nineteenth-century French critic, that the Gospel According to Luke is the most beautiful book in the world. That it is also the most joyful book even the casual reader can discover by turning its pages and observing how often the grace note is sounded there. Luke begins with "good tidings of great joy," the song of the angels announcing to the world the birth of the Savior. By chapter 15 the song turns into a symphony of great joy with the thrice-repeated theme, "Rejoice with me," reaching its climax in a magnificent father-and-son banquet. How else could the book close than with that same fundamental note sounded at the benediction of the ascending Lord: "They returned to Jerusalem with great joy, and were continually in the temple blessing God"?

Commentators have pointed out that this Gospel of joy is characterized by a remarkable unity and continuity. Its narrative is held together by means of a common meal occurring on various and sundry occasions and in all kinds of settings and company. Each occasion becomes the vehicle for deepening fellowship, instruction, insight, and commitment as the participants break bread together. Our devotions will be particularly attentive to these significant occasions of table-fellowship in Luke's joyous Gospel.

It was the Psalmist who first used the famous words which comprise our theme: "Thou preparest a table before me." Life had taught David the precious truth that the Lord was not only his shepherd but also his host—and, surprisingly, that his table had been prepared in the presence of his enemies. David never forgot the time he and his followers had been privileged to eat the bread of God's presence in the wilderness. Nor could he ever forget the day his warriors had risked so much to bring him a cup of water from the well at Bethlehem; "but he would not drink it, saying, 'This is not water, but the blood of the men who went in jeopardy of their lives.'" Our devotions on joy will not be unmindful of the enemies at and around the table-fellowship.

After a lifetime of study in the Gospels, Martin Kaehler concluded that they are not really "biographies with a tragic conclusion, but passion narratives with an extended introduction." So it is fitting as we move through portions of Luke's rich and joyous Gospel to tarry a few moments daily at the tables where our Lord sat with critic and companion—that he might feed our souls.

> *Here would I feed upon the bread of God,*
> *Here drink with thee the royal wine of heaven;*
> *Here would I lay aside each earthly load,*
> *Here taste afresh the calm of sin forgiven.*

LEVI'S FEAST

The Gracious Calling

AFTER THIS JESUS WENT OUT, AND SAW A TAX COLLECTOR, NAMED LEVI, SITTING AT THE TAX OFFICE; AND HE SAID TO HIM, "FOLLOW ME." AND HE LEFT EVERYTHING, AND ROSE AND FOLLOWED HIM.
Luke 5:27–28

This Gospel lesson reminds us that it is possible to lay up treasures on earth, but that it is also possible and necessary to lay up treasures in heaven. Levi is an unforgettable example of how that happens.

When Levi left home that morning for the tax office he hadn't the faintest notion that his life would take a radical turn of 180 degrees before the day was over. We tend to paint this well-known tax collector in somber colors as a greedy, grasping man and a big operator. Yet he may have been just an ordinary businessman, of average honesty, perhaps even of integrity. God has his own way of working faith, when and where and in whom he pleases. God just touched the tax collector on the shoulder one morning and that made all the difference. Suddenly Levi's life revolved around a new center. Things no longer seemed important, but persons did. The reason for the conversion? A loving Person had come into his life.

An old tale relates how two brothers disputing the title to a tract of land were intelligent enough to take their case to a wise rabbi for adjudication. "It's mine," claimed the one brother. "No," contended the other, "it belongs to me." The rabbi said he would have to take the dispute under advisement and ask the land itself to render judgment. After listening intently with one ear to the ground he arose and delivered his verdict: "The land tells me it belongs to neither of you, but that both of you belong to it."

"We are masters of that which we can let go of," said another wise man, "but we are mastered by what holds us in its grip."

By nature the human creature resembles a spider in that each of us sits in the center of our own carefully spun web, ready at any moment to move out in any direction and pounce upon any hapless victim that gets trapped in that web. Now a spider is always a spider, but a human being can be changed—like Levi. Conversion means that the converging lines focusing inward are reversed, turned outward into paths of service. The radical turn happens as we "let go" and let God have his way with us.

> *Take my life, and let it be*
> *Consecrated, Lord, to thee;*
> *Take my moments and my days,*
> *Let them flow in ceaseless praise. Amen.*

Heart Murmur

AND LEVI MADE HIM A GREAT FEAST IN HIS HOUSE . . . AND THE PHARISEES AND THEIR SCRIBES MURMURED. *Luke 5:29–30*

On best-seller lists in recent years has been a book of practical psychology entitled *I'm OK—You're OK.* It sets forth clearly and persuasively various approaches people make to each other. Sometimes the formula is expressed one way, sometimes another. When criticism is being voiced the formula reads: "I'm OK—but he (or she, or it) is not OK." When one is healthy-minded one learns to say: "I'm OK—you're OK."

Under the expert guidance of a well-trained counselor a group of pastors had worked through the book and its analyses of human interaction, and there was notable progress in learning self-acceptance and a growing willingness to take other persons as they wished to be taken. After the expert left, however, and the conversation turned to a discussion of denominational educational materials, the old familiar anvil chorus of condemnation began to be heard in a rousing refrain. When there was a lull for breath someone recalling the earlier experience together asked what level of analysis the group was now on. One honest person replied: "We're back where we've always been, saying, 'I'm OK but the stupid curriculum is not!' "

We hear that same murmur in today's Scripture. The Pharisees and their scribes complained about Levi's unwashed and unacceptable guests at the feast he was giving.

In the Bible, the tendency to "murmur" is not just accepted as a common trait of human cussedness. It is rather an expression of an unbelieving spirit, such as was manifested by the children of Israel in their desert wanderings on the way from bondage to freedom, or by the envious workers who grumbled at the goodness of their employer in paying the underemployed and disadvantaged a living wage. Biblically speaking, murmuring has serious consequences.

When a physician detects a heart murmur in a patient he does not dismiss it as something ordinary, to be expected; he takes it seriously as something that might call for open-heart surgery.

> *Lord, I would clasp thy hand in mine,*
> *Nor ever murmur nor repine;*
> *Content, whatever lot I see,*
> *Since 'tis my God that leadeth me. Amen.*

In the Presence of Mine Enemies

"WHY DO YOU EAT AND DRINK WITH TAX COLLECTORS AND SINNERS?" *Luke 5:30*

In Washington, D.C., there is a Social Register, the blue book that lists the names of socially acceptable persons in the area. If you are planning a glamorous dinner party, a glance at this "Who's Who" assures you that your guests are numbered among the socially elect. What a painful thing it must be for those who find themselves dropped from that book of life.

In Jesus' day the Pharisees had a little black book that was consulted whenever they were invited to dinner. It enabled them to see whether their fellow guests were acceptable, or to be shunned. Among the blacklisted were such socially undesirable people as gamblers, money-lenders, and pigeon-race promoters; also people whose vocations made it difficult if not impossible to observe the ceremonial law, such as shepherds, bath-house attendants, butchers, camel-drivers, and sailors. Even physicians and barbers, the professional blood-letters of the day, were excluded. Right up at the top of every such list were the despised tax collectors. Theirs was a threefold offense—personal greed, unpatriotic collaboration with the enemy, and the state of being religiously beyond the pale.

The Pharisees asked Jesus' disciples, "Why do you eat and drink with tax collectors and sinners?" but there can be no doubt that their question was really addressed to Jesus, and it was he who answered. His response was, to us, eminently reasonable: A doctor deals with people who have need of his help, so Jesus goes to those whose need is greatest. But there is more than meets the eye in this response. Pascal said once, "There are only two kinds of men: the righteous who believe themselves sinners, and the rest, sinners, who believe themselves righteous." This is one of the themes that runs through the entire Gospel of Luke. You find it stated in the parable of the Pharisee and the publican, in the parable of the prodigal son and his brother, and at another dinner party when Simon was host and a woman "sinner" the unexpected guest. At the Cross we see a sinner who became righteous, and the sinner who remained self-righteous to the end.

Lord Jesus, thou preparest a table before me in the presence of mine enemies. Anoint my head with the oil of gladness in thy redeeming fellowship. May my name be found at the last in the Lamb's Book of Life. Amen.

The New and the Old

JESUS TOLD THEM A PARABLE ALSO: "NO ONE TEARS A PIECE FROM A NEW GARMENT AND PUTS IT UPON AN OLD GARMENT; IF HE DOES, HE WILL TEAR THE NEW, AND THE PIECE FROM THE NEW WILL NOT MATCH THE OLD. AND NO ONE PUTS NEW WINE INTO OLD WINESKINS; IF HE DOES, THE NEW WINE WILL BURST THE SKINS AND IT WILL BE SPILLED, AND THE SKINS WILL BE DESTROYED. BUT NEW WINE MUST BE PUT INTO FRESH WINESKINS."   *Luke 5:36–38*

In these twin parables of the new patch and the old wineskins our Lord concludes the table talk at Levi's feast. One thing leads to another and Jesus not only defends the joyful spirit of his own followers as completely in keeping with bridegroom time; he goes on to warn against the futile effort of trying to mix the new spirit with the old forms. Trying to make the new life in Christ fit the old order is as absurd as cutting a piece out of a brand new garment to patch an old coat, or as frustrating as pouring new wine into dry, cracked wineskins, hoping somehow that the potent new vintage won't be too hard on the old system. Don't try it!

The message is not merely a homespun truth, ripe wisdom issuing from experience and observation. It partakes of the newness of the New Testament itself: "The old has passed away, behold the *new* has come." What's new? "A *new* covenant," not just a new edition of the old order of things. "A *new* commandment give I to you." "We wait for *new* heavens and a *new* earth in which righteousness dwells."

5

No wonder Christ's first miracle at Cana rang the changes on the six empty waterpots set there for the rites of purification; their water was turned by the power and presence of the Lord into the new wine of the kingdom. And from that abundance, as an old church father once remarked, we still drink.

> *Finish then thy new creation,*
> *Pure and spotless let us be;*
> *Let us see thy great salvation*
> *Perfectly restored in thee!   Amen.*

SIMON'S PARTY

The Little More—And Oh, How Much It Is

ONE OF THE PHARISEES ASKED HIM TO EAT WITH HIM, AND JESUS WENT INTO THE PHARISEE'S HOUSE, AND SAT AT TABLE. AND BEHOLD, A WOMAN OF THE CITY, WHO WAS A SINNER, WHEN SHE LEARNED THAT HE WAS SITTING AT TABLE IN THE PHARISEE'S HOUSE, BROUGHT AN ALABASTER FLASK OF OINTMENT, AND STANDING BEHIND HIM AT HIS FEET, WEEPING, SHE BEGAN TO WET HIS FEET WITH HER TEARS, AND WIPED THEM WITH THE HAIR OF HER HEAD, AND KISSED HIS FEET, AND ANOINTED THEM WITH THE OINTMENT.

Luke 7:36–38

Four hundred years ago Martin Luther commented about Luke's story of Simon and the woman who was a sinner. "This is a most excellent story which ought to be preached on every year, for it holds up for us to see the two chief points of Christian doctrine, namely, what true repentance is and how one obtains forgiveness of sins."

It started out as a low-key dinner party given by Simon the Pharisee for a certain young rabbi who happened to be passing through town and stopped over for the synagogue service. Simon knew that courtesy required hospitality to be extended to strangers. He was a low-key person himself, and felt that the occasion did not require him to go all out. The best china stayed in the cupboard and there was no need to polish the sterling service. Flowers for the table were conspicuous by their absence, and the welcome extended the visitor was adequate but nothing to get excited about.

Suddenly the air became electric. In those days it was common for visitors to drop in uninvited, the poor hoping for a handout, the curious for a bit of excitement in their drab days. But who would ever dream of seeing a woman who was a sinner coming into respectable company? Simon just did not know what to make of her emotional display, her tears, her impulsive kisses planted on Jesus' feet. Did she think he was a king as she anointed him with oil?

Jesus had something to say to the woman, but he felt impelled to deal first of all with Simon's sins of omission. He reminded him of the neglected courtesies—no water for his dusty feet, no kiss of courtesy, no oil in token of the amenities of life. "You think of her in terms of torrid sin, of passion and wanton physical excess. Fire consumes but ice will also suffice to destroy." Wordsworth spoke of "that best portion of a good man's life—those little, nameless, unremembered acts of kindness and of love."

Lord, open my eyes too. Make me aware. Share with me thy compassion for others who are different from me, and awaken me to my own need to be forgiven. Amen.

Having a Past—And a Future

NOW WHEN THE PHARISEE WHO HAD INVITED JESUS SAW IT, HE SAID TO HIMSELF, "IF THIS MAN WERE A PROPHET, HE WOULD HAVE KNOWN WHO AND WHAT SORT OF WOMAN THIS IS WHO IS TOUCHING HIM, FOR SHE IS A SINNER."

Luke 7:39

The disturbing thing was that Jesus *did* realize what sort of woman was standing behind him. Simon had not said it out loud. He is one of those characters in Scripture who talks to himself. But there is such a thing as body language and even a novice could read what Simon was saying by it. His back was turned to her, his whole body was held stiffly aloof, his nostrils pinched as though some foul odor had come into the room with her. Simon wondered about Jesus, but he didn't have to wait long. Like Nathanael under the fig tree and the Samaritan at the well, Simon discovered that he was in the presence of One who knew what was in man.

Simon had said, "She is a sinner." He would have volunteered that the particular pigeon hole of her sinful proclivities had to do with sex. Most people think that way today. But scholars have pointed out that the Pharisees did not just disdain and condemn women who were adulteresses; they stoned them!

For Jesus, however, the most important fact about a person is not his past, but that under God he or she has a future. When John Wesley lay on his deathbed, his friends bent over him to hear his last counsel, the rich harvest of the years. All he said was, "I am the chief of sinners, but Jesus died for me." Martin Luther's great discovery was that the Christian's whole life is a daily repentance, daily confession, daily absolution, daily renewal. Paul's one great hope was that he could "forget what lies behind and strain forward to what lies ahead."

This woman's only hope was that "her sins, which are many, are forgiven." The verb form Jesus uses is the perfect passive; it means that something is now past and finished but continues to have present meaning because God has acted once and for all. Simon and the woman both had a past; the woman had a future. Forgiveness makes that kind of a difference.

> O thou, to whose all searching sight
> The darkness shineth as the light,
> Search, prove my heart; it pants for thee;
> O burst these bonds, and set it free.   Amen.

Something to Say

AND JESUS ANSWERING SAID TO HIM, "SIMON, I HAVE SOMETHING TO SAY. . . . A CERTAIN CREDITOR HAD TWO DEBTORS; ONE OWED FIVE HUNDRED DENARII, AND THE OTHER FIFTY. WHEN THEY COULD NOT PAY, HE FORGAVE THEM BOTH. NOW WHICH OF THEM WILL LOVE HIM MORE?" SIMON ANSWERED,

"THE ONE, I SUPPOSE, TO WHOM HE FORGAVE MORE." AND HE
SAID TO HIM, "YOU HAVE JUDGED RIGHTLY." *Luke 7:40–43*

Have you ever noticed how many of the parables of Jesus
deal with contrasts and comparisons between two sorts of
people? By a stroke of genius a medieval dramatist com-
bined the characters of two different parables, with devastat-
ing effect. In his play the elder brother in the parable of the
prodigal son played the part of the Pharisee in the parable of
the Pharisee and the publican. Of course the prodigal son
played the part of the publican. It was the occasion of
the ne'er-do-well brother's return that produced that self-
righteous prayer in the temple, as the Pharisee/elder brother
gave thanks that he had never fallen so low. Besides being
good theater it showed profound religious insight.

The dramatist could have gone on with the same characters
in the parable of the two debtors. Simon would have ob-
jected to the allegation that he owed God anything because,
if anything, he felt that he had a credit balance with the
Almighty. The forgiven sinner, on the other hand, finds her
cup of joy running over in awareness of the wideness of God's
mercy. Simon finds little room for gratitude because he
lacked awareness of "how little worthy of any love thou art!"

"Alas," cries John Bunyan, "Christ has but little thanks for
the saving of little sinners. He gets not water for his feet by
his saving such sinners. There are an abundance of dry-eyed
Christians in the world, and an abundance of dry-eyed duties
too: duties that were never wetted with the tears of contri-
tion and repentance, nor even sweetened with the great sinner's box of ointment."

> But drops of grief can ne'er repay
>   The debt of love I owe.
> Here, Lord, I give myself away;
>   'Tis all that I can do.   Amen.

"Sins? Sins? I Haven't Any!"

"THEREFORE I TELL YOU, HER SINS, WHICH ARE MANY, ARE
FORGIVEN, FOR SHE LOVED MUCH."   *Luke 7:47*

Words, like people, have a life span of their own. Some
die aborning. Others, like Methusaleh, live on toward the
millennium, but eventually even they, like Yeats' human
scarecrow, "tattered coat upon a stick," finally topple into
graves marked by the lexicographer's sign: "Obs.," meaning
obsolete. Would it astonish you to learn that "forgiveness"
in the dictionary is marked thus in two of its meanings?

It does not require the services of a Sherlock Holmes to
discover that A. Conan Doyle was right when he said, "Modern man isn't worrying very much about his sins." How
many politicians have been forced to admit that they have
done wrong, or made mistakes, from the best of motives, of
course? But when have you heard a politician coming clean
like the prodigal son and saying, "I have *sinned* against
heaven and before you; I am no longer worthy to be called
your son"?

This obsolescence or at least a decline in the sense of sin is
found even in the church. An Anglican theologian remembers how annoyed his great aunt was by her husband's predi-
lection for sermons on the subject of sin. She came home
from church one Sunday and ventilated her frustration to a
member of the family. "Sins? Sins? I haven't got any sins!
Only your uncle annoys me sometimes." Why did he preach
on sin? Why do church worship orders keep talking about us
"poor, miserable sinners"? Poor she was, miserable she wasn't,
and she pleaded "not guilty" to the charge of being a sinner.

Surprisingly this atrophy is found in the Roman Catholic
Church too. Ronald Knox commented once on the anomaly
that whereas four hundred years ago it was difficult to persuade people that any sins were venial, in these days it is seem-

ingly impossible to persuade anyone that any sins are mortal.

And that brings us to ourselves. If we were completely honest we would probably say with a good conscience, "Sins? Sins? I haven't any sins! But people like this woman here annoy me no end!"

> I need thee, precious Jesus!
> For I am full of sin;
> My soul is dark and guilty,
> My heart is dead within.

Come into my life, Lord Jesus. Stab my spirit broad awake until I know my need of thy pardoning grace. Amen.

Are We Still Friends?

"HER SINS, WHICH ARE MANY, ARE FORGIVEN."   Luke 7:47

What transpired that day between the woman and Jesus is unknown to us. Perhaps she had been present when he told the story of the boy who finally came to himself and went home to discover that his father was even more eager to have his son back than the son was to get back. More important to the father was the restoring of broken ties than the punishing of past sins. Now with the help of his father he could work out the problems of a misspent past.

One of the most profound sayings Martin Luther ever uttered sprang from this same discovery: "Sinners are not loved because they are lovely; rather, they are lovely because they are loved." The woman could love now because she knew that God loved her and forgave her. On the other hand, Simon her host was the epitome of lovelessness, "faultily faultless, icicly regular, splendidly null."

A seven-year-old son had been rebelliously naughty and had to be punished. To underscore the seriousness of the misdeed his father marched the lad off to bed without supper. Later that evening the study door opened and the little offender stood in the doorway. "What are you doing down here?" the father demanded sternly. "You're supposed to be in bed." "But Daddy," cried the boy, "I've got to ask a question." "What?" "What I've got to know is, are we still friends?"

If the father-son relationship was still intact, all was still well. That is what Jesus came to tell us. With Jesus as friend, the past loses its power to haunt, and the future is bright with hope.

> One there is above all others,
>   Well deserves the name of Friend:
> His is love above a brother's,
>   Costly, free, and knows no end;
> They who once his kindness prove
> Find it everlasting love.   Amen.

A Grateful Heart

"YOU GAVE ME NO KISS, BUT FROM THE TIME I CAME IN SHE HAS NOT CEASED TO KISS MY FEET. YOU DID NOT ANOINT MY HEAD WITH OIL, BUT SHE HAS ANOINTED MY FEET WITH OINTMENT. . . . HE WHO IS FORGIVEN LITTLE, LOVES LITTLE."

Luke 7:45–47

In "The Hound of Heaven," one of the great religious poems on the theme of man's flight and God's unending pursuit, Francis Thompson tells how God outran, outloved him, and he heard these words:

> 'Strange, piteous, futile thing!
> Wherefore should any set thee love apart?
> Seeing none but I makes much of naught' (He said),
> 'And human love needs human meriting:
>   How hast thou merited—
> Of all man's clotted clay the dingiest clot?
>   Alack, thou knowest not
> How little worthy of any love thou art!
> Whom wilt thou find to love ignoble thee
>   Save Me, save only Me?'

13

For Thompson that was the end and also the beginning of faith, hope, and gratitude.

Martin Luther wrote his exposition of the Magnificat in a time of strain and deep trouble, with his very life hanging in the balance most of the time. In the treatise Luther tells of a shepherd lad standing beside the road weeping as though his heart would break. A cardinal, riding by, desired to offer comfort and asked the reason for his tears. The lad was a long time ceasing his sobbing, but at last he pointed to an ugly toad sitting on the ground. "I weep," he said, "because God has made me so well favored a creature and not hideous like this reptile, but I have never until now acknowledged it, or thanked and praised him therefor." The cardinal rode off, shaking his head, and saying, "This shepherd was neither rich nor comely nor powerful; nevertheless he had so clear an insight into God's good gifts, and pondered them so deeply, that he found therein more than he could comprehend."

You and I are "ransomed, healed, restored, forgiven." Who like us his praise should sing? Gratitude is what it all comes down to.

O God, thou hast given us so much. Grant us yet this one thing more—a grateful heart. Amen.

The Price of Pardon

AND HE SAID TO HER, "YOUR SINS ARE FORGIVEN." *Luke 7:48*

It is precisely here that thoughtful people have difficulty with forgiveness. It is all very well to tell this woman she is forgiven. It is gracious to welcome home the prodigal. But what about the past? "The moving finger writes, and having writ, moves on. Nor all your piety nor all your wit, can lure it back to cancel half a line of it!" Other lives had been marred by her sin, perhaps scarred beyond repair. Even a creditor, when remitting a great debt, cannot just write off the debt. Someone has to pay. So George Bernard Shaw complained that "forgiveness is a coward's refuge!" A man must pay his own bills!

But Jesus' well-known parable of the two debtors says of both, "They could not pay." What then? P. T. Forsyth wrestled with this problem and gave his answer in an old story about a semi-barbarian leader named Schamyl who found his plans to fight his tribal enemy frustrated again and again because someone always revealed his plans to the enemy. Schamyl sternly decreed that, if found, the guilty person would be unmercifully flogged in public. But when the truth finally came to light it was revealed that it was his own mother who was guilty. What should he do? He secluded himself in his tent for two days, then emerged and told his men to strip him, bind him, and scourge him instead of his mother.

But this only complicates our problem. Is God a blood-thirsty deity exacting blood and tears from his Son to atone for our sins? We find ourselves reacting as did the child who rejected that kind of atonement theory by saying, "I love Jesus, but I hate God." Yet suffering love seems to be the only way, even for God. "Forgiveness," said Martin Luther, "is a knot that needs God's help to unravel." In the Cross we see how God dealt with the problem.

> Glory be to Jesus,
>   Who, in bitter pains,
> Poured for me the life-blood
>   From his sacred veins!
>
> Grace and life eternal
>   In that Blood I find;
> Blest be his compassion,
>   Infinitely kind.   Amen.

THE PHARISEE'S LUNCHEON

The Pure in Heart

WHILE JESUS WAS SPEAKING, A PHARISEE ASKED HIM TO DINE WITH HIM; SO HE WENT IN AND SAT AT TABLE. THE PHARISEE WAS ASTONISHED TO SEE THAT HE DID NOT FIRST WASH BEFORE DINNER. AND THE LORD SAID TO HIM, "NOW YOU PHARISEES CLEANSE THE OUTSIDE OF THE CUP AND OF THE DISH, BUT INSIDE YOU ARE FULL OF EXTORTION AND WICKEDNESS. YOU FOOLS! DID NOT HE WHO MADE THE OUTSIDE MAKE THE INSIDE ALSO?" *Luke 11:37–40*

"Save the surface and you save all" is an excellent slogan for paint manufacturers. Wood siding exposed to the elements without the protection of paint deteriorates rapidly. Bridges with exposed steel girders are particularly susceptible to rust and corrosion. Often on a large bridge, when the painters finish a paint job, to "save the surface" they immediately go back to the beginning and start all over again.

But Jesus cannot be content with such a slogan in the religious realm. Invited to dinner one noon he made a point of flouting the ritualistic ablution of his hands. He took the occasion to speak plainly about the discrepancy between the way opponents zealously scrubbed their hands and the way they at the same time messed up their internal affairs by hypocrisy, greed, and all sorts of other thoughts that could not stand the light of day. Jesus was no muckraker like that character John Bunyan who, spiritually, could make no "pilgrim's progress" because "he could look no way but downwards, with a muckrake in his hand." Jesus knew that if you save the heart, the inner man, you save all.

When Ulysses and his men were sailing past the dangerous isles where the seductive maidens of Circe had sung many a sailor to his death, to combat temptation he plugged everyone else's ears with wax and had his men bind him to the mast, far from the tiller. Even so, the passage proved difficult and taxing. Yet when Orpheus, the divine musician, passed those same unholy isles, he did not even hear the seductive songs. He was playing divine music himself.

Not willpower but Christ's power, the expulsive power of a new affection, makes the heart clean within and able to overcome the foe without.

> Grant my mind and my affections
> Wisdom, counsel, purity,
> That I may be ever seeking
> Naught but that which pleases thee.
> Let thy knowledge spread and grow,
> Working error's overthrow. Amen.

On Giving All

"BUT WOE TO YOU PHARISEES! FOR YOU TITHE MINT AND RUE AND EVERY HERB, AND NEGLECT JUSTICE AND THE LOVE OF GOD."   Luke 11:42

One subject on which you can easily generate more heat than light is stewardship in general, and tithing in particular. In this regard the unhappy luncheon Luke talks about here was no exception. Where would the fellowship of faith be without the person who tithes—and makes tithing only a base from which to move on to larger and more sacrificial offerings? Anyone who has ever stood in King's College Chapel remembers with gratitude the royal saint and his visionary architect who joined hands to erect that house of prayer, a thing of beauty and a joy forever. Wordsworth caught the spirit of gratitude in his memorable lines: "Give all thou canst; high heaven rejects the lore, of nicely calculated less or more." The people of God need that reminder in days of shrinking gifts.

Our Lord's problem with the folks he was talking to was not that they were committed to tithing, even to the extent of tithing the produce of their herb gardens, but that they neglected the costly and more weighty matters pertaining to justice toward their fellow human beings and love toward God. The charge is still true. I for one can certainly plead guilty to a myopic scrupulosity about trivia, and neglect of the mighty causes in our day that cry out for justice and mercy.

> We give thee but thine own,
>   Whate'er the gift may be;
> All that we have is thine alone,
>   A trust, O Lord, from thee.
>
> May we thy bounties thus
>   As stewards true receive,
> And gladly, as thou blessest us,
>   To thee our first-fruits give.   Amen.

Praise Comes Well

"WOE TO YOU PHARISEES! FOR YOU LOVE THE BEST SEATS IN THE SYNAGOGUES AND SALUTATIONS IN THE MARKET PLACES."   *Luke 11:43*

The best seats and respectful salutations—let's face it—how we love them! Robert James McCracken tells of the occasion when he was invited back to Canada as Good Friday preacher in Ottawa. The humble Highland Scot thought how wonderful it would be if his mother could only see him now. His cup of joy ran over when the governor general's equerry waited on him after the service with an invitation to Government House. In the midst of the formalities he became a bit concerned about making his train, but then he relaxed as the mounted police escort parted the traffic before him like Moses opening the way for the Israelites at the Red Sea. Sinking back in his Pullman seat and receiving the salute of the man in the red coat just as the train moved majestically out of the station, he wondered if anybody had seen all the ceremony and grandeur. Then, almost audibly, he heard the rebuke, "And you, the Good Friday preacher!"

John Henry Jowett never forgot the day he went to Water Street Mission to preach. A layman introduced him as "the Dr. Jowett who needed no introduction," and then prayed, "We thank you Lord for sending our brother here today. Now blot him out so that we can hear what you have to say." Dr. Jowett needed that, and confessed that he was singularly assisted in the pulpit that day.

Praise has always been comely to the upright! In Zoar Street Chapel John Bunyan drew such crowds that he had to be lifted over the heads of the congregation to get to the pulpit. "What a sweet sermon you gave," said an admirer— who was unprepared for the response: "I know; the devil told me of it before I was out of the pulpit."

We pray in the words of John Bunyan:

> He that is down needs fear no fall,
>   He that is low, no pride;
> He that is humble ever shall
>   Have God to be his guide.
>
> Fulness to such a burden is
>   That go on pilgrimage;
> Here little, and hereafter bliss
>   Is best from age to age. Amen.

All or Nothing

"WOE TO YOU! FOR YOU ARE LIKE GRAVES WHICH ARE NOT SEEN, AND MEN WALK OVER THEM WITHOUT KNOWING IT."
Luke 11:44

The third "woe" in this series of seven reminds one of the words in the book of Revelation about the church in Sardis:

"I know your works; you have the name of being alive, and you are dead." In Jesus' day it was customary to mark graves with chalk to warn the unwary against contaminating touch. Jesus says that faith is either a grave or grace, either dead or alive.

Henrik Ibsen attacked the social shams of his time with plays like *The Doll's House* and *The Master Builder*. In *Brand* he attacked the cheap-grace religion of his fellow Norwegians. A firebrand pastor named Brand holds up to scorn the image his people have of God not as father but as grandfather, indulgent and benign. Brand refuses his own mother a death-bed absolution because she will not make full restitution of funds she filched from a dying relative. God demands "all or nothing!" She dies unshriven. Brand breaks his wife's heart with the same unyielding demand when their little Isaac is sacrificed upon the altar of what the pastor considers to be the will of God.

In the play's final act, Brand follows a demented creature up the mountainside to the ice chapel promised to all-or-nothing believers. Brand sees an avalanche plunging down the mountain and knows it will bury him alive. Like a drowning man seeing his whole life telescoped into a single moment, he realizes that his religion has been hate not love, guts not grace, self-will not God's will. He dies shaking his fist in God's face. As the curtain falls a voice is heard from heaven proclaiming, "God is love."

Since I must choose betweeen the way of life or the way of death, help me to choose the way marked by thy redeeming cross.

> *Just as I am, without one plea,*
> *But that thy Blood was shed for me,*
> *And that thou bidd'st me come to thee,*
> *   O Lamb of God, I come, I come.   Amen.*

On Burden-Bearing

ONE OF THE LAWYERS ANSWERED HIM, "TEACHER, IN SAY-
ING THIS YOU REPROACH US ALSO." AND JESUS SAID, "WOE
TO YOU LAWYERS ALSO! FOR YOU LOAD MEN WITH BURDENS
HARD TO BEAR, AND YOU YOURSELVES DO NOT TOUCH THE
BURDENS WITH ONE OF YOUR FINGERS." *Luke 11:45–46*

Lawyers in the first century were not attorneys so much as
they were the Supreme Court in religious affairs. They were
professional theologians while their colleagues, the Pharisees,
were laymen and practitioners. The lawyer reproaches Jesus
for his reproach of them. The root of the word for reproach
is *"hybris,"* which for many educated people of the day was
the sin of sins, a sin calculated to bring down upon the proud
offender's head the wrath of the gods. Jesus lets the charge
stand because he saw his opponents presuming to pervert
religion into a burden laid on those least able to bear it.

An old rabbinic tale relates that Moses smashed the stone
tables containing the commandments of God; he broke them
into fragments. Seeking souvenirs, some rushed up and got
bits that said "kill," "steal," "covet," but the poor people
who had to take what was left got only the words "thou shalt
not." It took a lawyer to sort out the manifold precepts of
the time—613 as the law was then understood—but Jesus
reduced God's whole demand to just two facets: love of God
and love of neighbor. Martin Luther made it three (or one):
fear, love, and trust in God above all things. To people who
found the religious requirements and restrictions a burden
laid upon a burden, Jesus came with an offer that it would
be folly to reject: "Come to me, all who labor and are heavy
laden, and I will give you rest. Take my yoke upon you,
and learn from me; for I am gentle and lowly in heart, and
you will find rest for your souls. For my yoke is easy, and
my burden is light."

Lord, thou hast commanded us to cast our burden upon thee. We have found it such a burden as wings are to a bird, or sails to a ship. Make us burden-bearers for the weary, the heavy-laden. Amen.

Like Father Like Son

"WOE TO YOU! FOR YOU BUILD THE TOMBS OF THE PROPHETS WHOM YOUR FATHERS KILLED. SO YOU ARE WITNESSES AND CONSENT TO THE DEEDS OF YOUR FATHERS; FOR THEY KILLED THEM, AND YOU BUILD THEIR TOMBS." *Luke 11:47–48*

What a strange perversity of human nature Jesus exposes here! His generation made quite a cult of hero worship. They lavished money on tombs and monuments to the prophets whose message had been rejected by their fathers, and whose blood they had shed. But this had all become Israel's sacred heritage. Tours and pilgrimages to sacred places were organized as avidly then as they are now to Mount Vernon, Monticello, Rome, or Geneva. Must it always take generations to turn a heresy into a heritage?

The Eternal Road was the name Franz Werfel gave to a play in which he held the mirror of the past up to the people of his day. A group of Jews fleeing from a mob take refuge in their synagogue. While waiting for the mob to grow weary and leave, the rabbi takes the scroll of Scripture from the tabernacle and begins to read. As his voice drones on the lights fade, and when they come up again the same Jews in twentieth-century Europe reappear on the road of history as grumblers, as weak and timorous, but a few are seen as the remnant of the faithful. Like the promised One this holy remnant "endured as seeing the invisible."

In this latest "woe" Jesus is saying in effect: "As it was in the beginning, it is now, and ever shall be." A tomb is in the process of building; his proclamation is to be interred along with all that is mortal of the man. Jesus is foretelling his own fate. Somewhere soon these sons of the fathers will bury him too and reject his message.

O God, unto whom all hearts are open, help us to look into the mirror of thy word. Save us from the sin of blindness to thy presence, and bring us to true repentance and faith ere the day of grace is over. Amen.

The Key of Knowledge

"WOE TO YOU LAWYERS! FOR YOU HAVE TAKEN AWAY THE KEY OF KNOWLEDGE; YOU DID NOT ENTER YOURSELVES, AND YOU HINDERED THOSE WHO WERE ENTERING." *Luke 11:52*

The seventh and last "woe" is pronounced by Jesus upon the leaders of religion who obstruct knowledge among the people, who lock up the Book of Life and throw away the key. Always there have been seers like Harriet Beecher Stowe who perceived the Lord "trampling out the vintage where the grapes of wrath are stored." Lincoln too in his time was a clear-eyed seer. Our Lord saw in the impending events God's visitation upon the faithless and disobedient from the days when Abel's blood was shed by his jealous brother to the last martyr named in the Second Book of the Chronicles, with which the Hebrew Bible ended.

In our day we have again come to the end of an era. The time is critical for every believer, every custodian of the message. To the teacher, and especially the theologian, to the historian and everyone to whom God has entrusted his store of knowledge for proclamation comes the cry of warning: "Woe to you if you fail to open the book to the people of God."

O thou who openest and no man shuts, and shuts and no man opens, enables us to keep thy word and not deny thy name. By our faithfulness may all who seek find the ever-open door. Amen.

A RULER'S DINNER

To Keep It Holy

ONE SABBATH WHEN JESUS WENT TO DINE AT THE HOUSE OF
A RULER WHO BELONGED TO THE PHARISEES, THEY WERE
WATCHING HIM. AND BEHOLD, THERE WAS A MAN BEFORE
HIM WHO HAD DROPSY. AND JESUS SPOKE TO THE LAWYERS
AND PHARISEES, SAYING, "IS IT LAWFUL TO HEAL ON THE
SABBATH, OR NOT?" BUT THEY WERE SILENT. THEN HE TOOK
HIM AND HEALED HIM, AND LET HIM GO. AND HE SAID TO
THEM, "WHICH OF YOU, HAVING AN ASS OR AN OX THAT HAS
FALLEN INTO A WELL, WILL NOT IMMEDIATELY PULL HIM OUT
ON A SABBATH DAY?" AND THEY COULD NOT REPLY TO THIS.

Luke 14:1–6

A recent newspaper cartoon pictured a man looking up
from the sports page and saying to his wife, "It says here
that national football is going to be expanded even further."
Then he added, "There goes what was left of Sunday."

What is permitted on the sabbath/Sunday has been dis-
cussed for a long time. We have seen the gradual erosion of
the "day of all the days the best" from holy day to holiday,
from sabbath to Sunday, from Lord's Day to the secularized,
amusement-centered, anything-goes weekend.

Although in Jesus' day cooking was not permitted on the
sabbath, feasting was allowed. It was a family day, a synagogue day, a day when the rabbi was invited and people
heard him gladly. But this gathering which found Jesus dining at the house of a ruler was different.

A man afflicted with dropsy was there, his presence obviously rigged. Jesus met the challenge head-on by asking if
it was permitted to heal on the sabbath, a question the Pharisees refused to answer. Again, said he, if a child or an ani-

mal fell into a well they would not discuss theoretical questions but go at once into action. A man with dropsy was a child of God, fallen into the bottomless well which the word dropsy implies.

Jesus' own attitude was that God's work, life-giving and life-saving, was not only permitted but required at all times. The principle still applies today.

In our remembrance of the sabbath day, O Lord, help us to keep it holy in worship and thanksgiving, in healing and caring, in sharing and serving. Amen.

On Finding Your Place

NOW JESUS TOLD A PARABLE TO THOSE WHO WERE INVITED, WHEN HE MARKED HOW THEY CHOSE THE PLACES OF HONOR, SAYING TO THEM, "WHEN YOU ARE INVITED BY ANY ONE TO A MARRIAGE FEAST, DO NOT SIT DOWN IN A PLACE OF HONOR, LEST A MORE EMINENT MAN THAN YOU BE INVITED BY HIM; AND HE WHO INVITED YOU BOTH WILL COME AND SAY TO YOU, 'GIVE PLACE TO THIS MAN,' AND THEN YOU WILL BEGIN WITH SHAME TO TAKE THE LOWEST PLACE." *Luke 14:7–9*

When the Prince of Wales visited Vienna he asked particularly to see the palace where the Congress of Vienna made a fragile peace after the wars of Napoleon. The palace had been chosen for one reason, he was told: It had five doors leading to the main hall so that each ambassador could enter simultaneously with the other four, and nobody had to be second in taking his place at the peace table!

What Jesus saw at the ruler's house that day was a disorderly scramble as the dining room doors were thrown open and everybody rushed for the choice seats. Apparently one crestfallen guest had to be asked to go down lower so that the guest of honor might be seated properly.

Parables usually have one main thrust, and the thrust of Jesus' message is that everybody has a place at God's table.

25

We cannot all sit at the speaker's table, but we can all sit somewhere and share in God's bounty. The world says, "I'm a better man than you, have more brains, more money, more of this and that, so by rights I sit at the speaker's table." Christians say, "You're as good as I am. God loves us both, and place is relatively unimportant."

> *Jesus, what didst thou find in me*
> *That thou hast dealt so lovingly?*
> *How great the joy that thou hast brought,*
> *So far exceeding hope or thought!*
> *Jesus, my Lord, I thee adore,*
> *O make me love thee more and more.   Amen.*

The Grace of Humility

"BUT WHEN YOU ARE INVITED, GO AND SIT IN THE LOWEST PLACE, SO THAT WHEN YOUR HOST COMES HE MAY SAY TO YOU, 'FRIEND, GO UP HIGHER'; THEN YOU WILL BE HONORED IN THE PRESENCE OF ALL WHO SIT AT TABLE WITH YOU."

Luke 14:10

This passage sounds like a calculating, prudential bit of advice, but if that's all it is it would be out of character for Jesus, entirely different from all we know from Scripture of the mind of Christ. Perhaps there is more to it than meets the eye. Perhaps it means: the bigger the person the humbler he is, knowing that whatever one's gifts they are endowments, a trust to be used in the service of God and his people; the rest, the applause and the acclaim, do not matter.

Beethoven, who was no mean musician himself, was listening once to Bach's Mass in B Minor, the epitome of religious music. Beethoven turned to a friend and with a play on the master's name said, "You know he shouldn't be called Mr. Brook [Bach], he deserves to be called Mr. Ocean."

Yet for most of his career Bach could well have applied to himself Shakespeare's lament: "When, in disgrace with fortune and men's eyes, I all alone beweep my outcaste state, and trouble deaf heaven with my bootless cries. . . ." But he didn't. He just sat at his desk composing, or playing the organ for the divine service at St. Thomas Church in Leipzig. People ignored him, but with the help of Jesus he kept writing to the very end, dedicating his works "to the glory of God." Bach died as he lived, "unknown, unhonored, and unsung." They even forgot where he was buried, and his son could think of no better use for his father's musical manuscripts than selling them for a few small coins to the neighborhood butcher to wrap sausages in. Till one day God said, "Enough of that," and sent a young musician named Mendelssohn to say, "Friend, come up higher."

If our life is lived in God's service that's all that matters.

Father in heaven, thou hast put down the mighty from their seats and exalted those of low degree. Teach us the grace of humility and use us in thy service, for Jesus' sake. Amen.

Paid in Full

JESUS SAID ALSO TO THE MAN WHO HAD INVITED HIM, "WHEN YOU GIVE A DINNER OR A BANQUET . . . INVITE THE POOR, THE MAIMED, THE LAME, THE BLIND, AND YOU WILL BE BLESSED, BECAUSE THEY CANNOT REPAY YOU. YOU WILL BE REPAID AT THE RESURRECTION OF THE JUST."   *Luke 14:12–14*

Jesus certainly had no objection to neighborhood get-togethers or even to church fellowship suppers. He just did not want our fellowship to stop with people who live on the same side of the tracks as we do.

The people Jesus singled out as preferred guests were the very people for whom the temple was considered off limits. The reason the lame man lay at the beautiful gate of the temple was that by virtue of David's decree in 2 Samuel 5:8 he was not permitted inside. There was simply no place in the religious communities of those days for "the lame, halt, blind, dumb." True religion according to Jesus, however, begins where the rest leave off.

One blustery winter day a housewife struggling with an unbalanced budget heard the doorbell ring and found two shivering ragged children standing on the front porch. They asked if she had any old papers. Her inclination was to say no and send them packing, but their ragged coats and sopping feet got the better of her, and she invited them in. She even insisted on their sipping a hot cup of cocoa in the kitchen while she was rounding up the discarded papers. She was unprepared for the one question the girl asked: "Lady, are you rich?" "Goodness, no," she replied. "But Lady," the boy chimed in, "your cups match your saucers." The two children left without saying thanks, but the woman's heart was strangely warmed. She understood for the first time what Jesus meant when he said, "It is more blessed to give than to receive."

In haunts of wretchedness and need, on shadowed thresholds dark with fears, from paths where hide the lures of greed, O compassionate Christ, may we catch the vision of thy tears. Amen.

A Sense for What Is Vital

"A MAN ONCE GAVE A GREAT BANQUET, AND INVITED MANY; AND AT THE TIME FOR THE BANQUET HE SENT HIS SERVANT TO SAY TO THOSE WHO HAD BEEN INVITED, 'COME; FOR ALL IS NOW READY.' BUT THEY ALL ALIKE BEGAN TO MAKE EXCUSES. THE FIRST SAID TO HIM, 'I HAVE BOUGHT A FIELD, AND I MUST GO OUT AND SEE IT; I PRAY YOU, HAVE ME EXCUSED.' AND ANOTHER SAID, 'I HAVE BOUGHT FIVE YOKE OF OXEN, AND I GO TO EXAMINE THEM; I PRAY YOU, HAVE MF EXCUSED.' AND ANOTHER SAID, 'I HAVE MARRIED A WIFE, AND THEREFORE I CANNOT COME.'" *Luke 14:16–20*

A family awoke one night to find their house engulfed in flames. There was only time to grab a few things and leap for dear life. They discovered later that in their panic they had tossed out the window things of little worth and left expensive valuables behind. Paul prayed for his friends to be given "a sense of what is vital." We need that too.

The excuse-makers who bypassed the banquet were wrong on two accounts. First, they misread the invitation. They thought they were being invited to something disagreeable instead of to a wedding. A minister bringing an elderly parishioner a gift of money was unable to get her to come to the door. She explained afterward that she had been there in the house all the time but didn't come out because she thought the person outside was the landlord come to demand the rent.

The invited guests who stayed away made also a second miscalculation. They thought they could take a rain check and say "not just now" to the invitation God was delivering to them in person.

To buy a field, to buy oxen to till the field more efficiently, even to get married are all good things. They may be God's will for man. But when business crowds God out, and a couple are so wrapped up in themselves that there is no room for Christ, the blessing turns into a curse. "Seek His kingdom, and these things shall be yours as well."

> Thus may we serve thee, gracious Lord!
>   Thus ever thine alone,
> Our souls and bodies given to thee,
>   The purchase thou hast won;
> Through evil or through good report
>   Still keeping by thy side.
> By life or death, in this poor flesh
>   Let Christ be magnified! Amen.

On Doing Next Best

"THEN THE HOUSEHOLDER IN ANGER SAID TO HIS SERVANT, 'GO OUT QUICKLY TO THE STREETS AND LANES OF THE CITY, AND BRING IN THE POOR AND MAIMED AND BLIND AND LAME.' AND THE SERVANT SAID, 'SIR, WHAT YOU HAVE COMMANDED HAS BEEN DONE, AND STILL THERE IS ROOM.' AND THE MASTER SAID TO THE SERVANT, 'GO OUT TO THE HIGHWAYS AND HEDGES, AND COMPEL PEOPLE TO COME IN, THAT MY HOUSE MAY BE FILLED. FOR I TELL YOU, NONE OF THOSE MEN WHO WERE INVITED SHALL TASTE MY BANQUET.' "

Luke 14:21–24

Oscar Wilde tells of a maiden aunt who moved into a rural English mansion and planned a magnificent garden party for the whole countryside. The gardens wore their best colors, the lawns were manicured, and even the fickle weather cooperated with cloudless skies. There was only one problem —nobody came. Feeling snubbed and rejected, the poor old soul went to bed and died shortly after of a broken heart. Only later did they discover why nobody came. She had forgotten to mail the invitations. They lay in a bottom drawer, addressed, sealed, and stamped but never mailed.

God sent his servant Jesus in person to say to the people, "Come, for all is now ready," but all he got for his pains from his chosen ones was excuses, excuses, excuses.

Yet the point of the parable is neither their reluctance to come, nor their evasiveness in responding, but God's immense resourcefulness in inviting. He did what was next best. There were plenty of people who would jump at the invitation, publicans like Levi, poor sinners like the nameless woman who was forgiven much and loved much. If the Lord's own people weren't interested, there were others not averse to accepting God's call, even as Johnny-come-latelies.

Religiously we are all second-class citizens, but does that matter really?

Not worthy, Lord, to gather up the crumbs
   With trembling hand, that from thy table fall,
A weary, heavy-laden sinner comes
   To plead thy promise and obey thy call.   Amen.

Constrained by Love

"AND THE MASTER SAID TO THE SERVANT, 'GO OUT TO THE
HIGHWAYS AND HEDGES, AND COMPEL PEOPLE TO COME IN.' "
                                                      Luke 14:23

In his autobiography C. S. Lewis tells how he became a
happy atheist, then a reluctant agnostic, and finally a belliger-
ent believer. No one who has read *Surprised by Joy* will ever
forget the account of his conversion when, admitting finally
that God was God, he surrendered, knelt, and prayed.   So
far from being "surprised by joy," Lewis admits that at the
time he would have escaped if possible, fearful that he was
losing his freedom and happiness.   The joy came later.   For
the rest of his days he learned increasingly to be grateful to
the love that would not let him go and compelled him to
enter the house of feasting and reconciliation.

An alcoholic complained to his pastor, "It seems to me
you will never leave me alone." "That's right," said the
pastor, "I never shall, not while we are both above ground."
That did it.   The bolted door flew open: "If I am worth that
much to him, I must be worth something to myself; I'll have
another try."   Compassion, and the persistent patience that
will not let go, is what the kingdom of God is all about.   Compel them to come in!

*Jesus, lover of my soul, in the midst of things which please for
the moment, and things which displease for the moment, give me
a sense for that which alone is important because it is eternal.
Amen.*

31

AT THE HOUSE OF ZACCHAEUS

Seeking to See

JESUS ENTERED JERICHO AND WAS PASSING THROUGH. AND
THERE WAS A MAN NAMED ZACCHAEUS; HE WAS A CHIEF TAX
COLLECTOR, AND RICH. AND HE SOUGHT TO SEE WHO JESUS
WAS, BUT COULD NOT, ON ACCOUNT OF THE CROWD.

Luke 19:1–3

The thing that Zacchaeus wanted to do more than anything else that day was to see Jesus. He failed, partly
because he was small of stature but mainly because the
people around Jesus prevented his coming near.

In one of Strindberg's plays there is a scene in which a
nurse of strong religious convictions tries to convert a captain who is convinced that he is an atheist. "Why is it," the
captain asks her, "that when you speak of God and love your
voice becomes hard and your eyes fill with hate?" What he
saw in her prevented him from seeing Christ.

One of the most gifted and sensitive minds of our time
belonged to Sean O'Casey, the Irish playwright. He grew
up in almost incredible poverty and hardship in a Dublin
slum. One Sunday his mother marched him off to enroll in
church school over his protests that it was raining too hard,
that his clothes were too shabby, and that his shoes had
holes. Since these things were necessities, Sean decided
even as he sloshed through the downpour to invoke divine
assistance with respect at least to the footgear. "O God,
give me a new pair of boots," he murmured as he hurried
along, only to be mocked by a well-dressed companion who
overtook him on his way to the house of Jesus. Young

Sean might as well have been in Jericho for all the notice the teacher took of the new scholar that first day. Poor, wretched, hungry for acceptance, he saw none, felt none, and never went back.

What was it Jesus said about offending "these little ones"? Something about a millstone. "He sought to see who Jesus was, but could not, on account of the crowd."

> I need thee, precious Jesus!
>   For I am full of sin;
>   My soul is dark and guilty,
>   My heart is dead within.   Amen.

Lost and Found

SO ZACCHAEUS RAN ON AHEAD AND CLIMBED UP INTO A SYCAMORE TREE TO SEE JESUS, FOR HE WAS TO PASS THAT WAY.   *Luke 19:4*

What a vivid picture Luke paints of Zacchaeus—a rich man but so poorly regarded that nobody in the vast crowd would budge an inch to let him in where he could see Jesus. Though Jesus later calls him a son of Abraham, there is good reason to call him a man without a country. As a col- laborator working hand-in-glove to raise revenues for sup- porting the occupation forces, Zacchaeus was neither Roman nor Jew. His ill-gotten wealth made him the most despised man in Jericho, and rejection begot resentment in his heart for which he tried to find a balm by even greater knavery.

Rich, friendless, Zacchaeus was also a desperate man. He had to see Jesus. Augustine knew that same quiet desper- ation and wrote of it at the beginning of his *Confessions:* "Thou hast created us for thyself, and restless is our heart until it rests in thee." The wheel of life needs a sustaining axle about which to revolve.

Then came the moment when time stood still. Zacchaeus caught a glimpse of Jesus, but Jesus saw him too. Jesus even knew his name, called him, insisted on coming to his house that very day, and so filled the vacuum in his heart.

But it is not Zacchaeus who engages our attention so much as Jesus. The climax of the story and indeed the summary of the Gospel of Luke is here in the final words of Jesus, "The Son of man came to seek and to save the lost."

In finding Zacchaeus, Jesus lost the crowd. Fraternizing with the man up in the tree meant that when Jesus reached his journey's end he would lose his own life on the crabbed tree of the cross. And that's the story of the gospel, my story and yours—lost and found.

> With broken heart and contrite sigh,
> A trembling sinner, Lord, I cry;
> Thy pardoning grace is rich and free:
> O God, be merciful to me.   Amen.

The New Life

AND ZACCHAEUS STOOD AND SAID TO THE LORD, "BEHOLD, LORD, THE HALF OF MY GOODS I GIVE TO THE POOR; AND IF I HAVE DEFRAUDED ANY ONE OF ANYTHING, I RESTORE IT FOURFOLD."   *Luke 19:8*

There was an Old Testament law that governed people like Zacchaeus. Exodus 22 provided that if a man stole an ox or a sheep he had to make a fourfold restitution, and if he could not make restitution he was to be sold into slavery. Tax-collecting was a business so tainted with corruption that Zacchaeus would have to give that up too if he hoped to be accepted in the religious community.

But Jesus, strangely, lays down no conditions for Zacchaeus's rehabilitation. There is no sawdust trail for the sinner to walk. Jesus doesn't even say a thing about repentance or penance. He just comes into the man's house as guest, enters into his heart as master, gives him a new direction to travel, and the great transformation is under way.

Zacchaeus realized that there was no way of completely canceling out his sinful, irrevocable past. The people he had obviously defrauded had scattered now to the four winds. He simply states that he will make whatever restitution he can, and fulfill the letter of the law.

But he does not stop there, for the love of Christ constrains him now: "Behold, Lord, the half of my goods I give to the poor." The word "my" is emphatic and genuine. Not all his lucre is filthy; some of it he has come by honestly. And he now knows that to live—and love—is to give, not take. His giving now is not to salve his conscience or to buy God's favor. Like Abraham, the friend of God, he seeks now to bless by sharing.

Luke tells of two famous tax collectors. One of them was Levi, who when Christ called arose, left all, and followed him; Levi was called out of the world, to be one of the Twelve. Zacchaeus is called to stay in the world and be an honest businessman—a vastly different vocation. The call to faith is a call to serve—in this world that God loves.

> *Take my silver and my gold,*
> *Not a mite would I withhold;*
> *Take my intellect, and use*
> *Every power as thou shalt choose.   Amen.*

Till I Come

AS THEY HEARD THESE THINGS, JESUS PROCEEDED TO TELL A PARABLE, BECAUSE HE WAS NEAR TO JERUSALEM, AND BECAUSE THEY SUPPOSED THAT THE KINGDOM OF GOD WAS TO

APPEAR IMMEDIATELY. HE SAID THEREFORE, "A NOBLEMAN WENT INTO A FAR COUNTRY TO RECEIVE KINGLY POWER AND THEN RETURN. CALLING TEN OF HIS SERVANTS, HE GAVE THEM TEN POUNDS, AND SAID TO THEM, 'TRADE WITH THESE TILL I COME.' "
                                                            Luke 19:11–13

It was only a day's journey from Jericho to Jerusalem and the disciples were as excited as children are on the night before Christmas. As Jesus entered Jericho that morning the blind man by the wayside had hailed him as the Lord's anointed. He had used the forbidden name, "Son of David," and had asked the boon that he might see the Christ with his own eyes, and his prayer was answered. Though the crowds had tried to hush the blind man's cry, Jesus had not silenced him as he had silenced others on previous occasions. Messianic fever was mounting to a high pitch. Tomorrow they would be in Jerusalem, and who could tell what would happen then? What Jesus had taught them to pray for, the coming of the kingdom, was shortly to be fulfilled.

They supposed that the kingdom of God was to appear immediately. How should he break the news that what was to come was not a crown but a cross?

In its long history Israel had to learn to cope with delay and disappointment, the postponement of the promise. Abraham went out, not knowing where he was going but trusting wholly in the promises of God, and again and again he had to learn to wait, to be patient. Jesus reminded them how the noble Archelaus had gone to far off Rome to receive kingly power and only after many days return to exercise it. Facing a protracted absence of their Lord, the disciples were to carry on with patient perseverance.

To us, the church of the redeemed, his word, until he comes again in power, is the same: learn to labor and to wait. "It is required in stewards, that a man be found faithful."

Thy kingdom come! on bended knee
   The passing ages pray;
And faithful souls have yearned to see
   On earth that kingdom's day.   Amen.

I Was Afraid

"THE FIRST CAME BEFORE HIM, SAYING, 'LORD, YOUR POUND
HAS MADE TEN POUNDS MORE.' AND HE SAID TO HIM, 'WELL
DONE, GOOD SERVANT! BECAUSE YOU HAVE BEEN FAITHFUL
IN A VERY LITTLE, YOU SHALL HAVE AUTHORITY OVER TEN
CITIES.' AND THE SECOND CAME, SAYING, 'LORD, YOUR
POUND HAS MADE FIVE POUNDS.' AND HE SAID TO HIM,
'AND YOU ARE TO BE OVER FIVE CITIES.' THEN ANOTHER
CAME, SAYING, 'LORD, HERE IS YOUR POUND, WHICH I KEPT
LAID AWAY IN A NAPKIN; FOR I WAS AFRAID OF YOU, BE-
CAUSE YOU ARE A SEVERE MAN.' "   *Luke 19:16–21*

In the physical world nature's law is "Grow or die."   In
the realm of spirit someone has said, "Standing still is going
back."   The hapless third servant was a timid soul.   He
knew that he had an austere master, but failed to realize he
would not let him get by with zero growth.

A pioneer missionary, his mission all but accomplished,
asked a friend how many people on the island were still not
professing Christians, and he was told there were seventeen.
"Thank God," he said.   "When I came there were only
seventeen who were Christians."

Statistics, mere numbers, are not that important, but as
long as the parable of the pounds is in the New Testament,
the Lord of the church looks to his servants for lives of
faithfulness.

   Keep us faithful; keep us pure;
      Keep us evermore thine own;
   Help, O help us to endure;
      Fit us for the promised crown.   Amen.

Faithful in Little

"WHEN HE RETURNED, HAVING RECEIVED KINGLY POWER, HE COMMANDED THESE SERVANTS, TO WHOM HE HAD GIVEN THE MONEY, TO BE CALLED TO HIM, THAT HE MIGHT KNOW WHAT THEY HAD GAINED BY TRADING." *Luke 19:15*

On three other occasions after dinner the table talk included one or more parables. Matthew at this point has the parable of the talents, while Luke recalls the less familiar parable of the pounds. A talent was a considerable sum of money, a truly royal trust, while the responsibility for administering a pound, the equivalent of twenty dollars, wouldn't keep a man awake nights.

What Jesus is saying is that every human being has a gift, and all of us, yes even the least of us, must do our part. How often do you run into an Einstein, a Beethoven, or a Barth? Someone has said that such people are like four-leaf clovers, but what really keeps the pastures green, the cows fed, and the bees happy is the vastly more numerous ordinary, run-of-the-mill, three-leaf variety.

God doesn't expect us to be virtuosos, but he does expect us to produce. He doesn't demand that we be shining success stories, but he does require his servants to be found faithful.

A man who volunteered for military service but was rejected for physical reasons was assigned a mute, inglorious job of guarding a railroad bridge against sabotage and an invasion that never materialized. He took a lot of good-natured chaffing, but his answer was, "I was there if needed."

Can the Lord count on us? Wherein will we have grown and gained before the day of reckoning?

Deliver us from sloth in thy work, O Lord, and all coldness in thy cause. Rekindle our love and renew our strength in thy service. Amen.

The Man Who Has

" 'I TELL YOU, THAT TO EVERY ONE WHO HAS WILL MORE BE
GIVEN; BUT FROM HIM WHO HAS NOT, EVEN WHAT HE HAS
WILL BE TAKEN AWAY. BUT AS FOR THESE ENEMIES OF MINE,
WHO DID NOT WANT ME TO REIGN OVER THEM, BRING THEM
HERE AND SLAY THEM BEFORE ME.' " *Luke 19:26-27*

Struggle with it as we will, Jesus here states a law of life
that is as unbreakable as the law of gravity: "Use it or lose
it!" There is no third possibility.

Charles Darwin ruefully confessed that his mind had
become a machine into which large collections of facts were
poured, and out of which in time proceeded general laws of
scientific application. At one time he had a poet's awareness
of another world altogether, a world of beauty and of art.
"Prior to the age of thirty," Darwin wrote, "poetry of many
kinds such as the works of Milton, Gray, Bunyan, Wordsworth, Coleridge, and Shelley gave me great pleasure. Even
as a boy I took intense delight in Shakespeare." Darwin had
to leave all that to one side when he entered the laboratory,
though he always promised himself one day he would return
to it and things would be different.

But ultimately he discovered, to his dismay, that he had
hardening of the appreciative faculties. "If I had my life
to live over again," he wrote, "I would make it a rule to read
a little poetry and hear a little music every week; for perhaps
the parts of my brain now atrophied would thus have been
kept active through use."

> O teach me, Lord, that I may teach
>   The precious things thou dost impart;
> And wing my words, that they may reach,
>   The hidden depths of many a heart. Amen.

THE LORD'S SUPPER

Come, Lord Jesus

NOW AS THEY WENT ON THEIR WAY, JESUS ENTERED A VIL-
LAGE; AND A WOMAN NAMED MARTHA RECEIVED HIM INTO
HER HOUSE. AND SHE HAD A SISTER CALLED MARY, WHO SAT
AT THE LORD'S FEET AND LISTENED TO HIS TEACHING. BUT
MARTHA WAS DISTRACTED WITH MUCH SERVING; AND SHE
WENT TO HIM AND SAID, "LORD, DO YOU NOT CARE THAT
MY SISTER HAS LEFT ME TO SERVE ALONE? TELL HER THEN
TO HELP ME."
Luke 10:38–40

The house at Bethany was special. Here lived that family
of three which meant so much to Jesus—Mary, Martha, and
their brother Lazarus, who strangely does not appear during
the brief encounter reported in Luke. It does not require
much imagination to understand Martha's anxiety: "Company
coming and nothing prepared. And look at the house. If
only he could have waited until Friday when the cleaning
was done. A hundred things to do, and only two hands!"
Martha was so busy rattling pans in the kitchen that she
failed to hear Jesus' gentle knocking at the door.

Martha never stopped to ask whether her plans and her
guest's desires coincided. She should have realized that with
criticism mounting and with foes closing in relentlessly on
him, Jesus had no heart for gourmet food. A minister-pro-
fessor who had suffered many things of many cooks once
asked, "Wherein does the essence of hospitality lie, in giving
your guest what you think he ought to want, or in giving
him what he does want?" The tone of Jesus' voice suggested
a loving rebuke: "Martha, Martha, you are anxious and
troubled about many things; few things are needful, or only

one." Jesus would have been satisfied with a platter or dish instead of a banquet.

Is this the way out of anxiety, to prefer the one to the many, the significant to the superficial? Can we be satisfied to be fed by his words instead of thinking we must feed him?

Come, Lord Jesus, be our guest, and let these gifts to us be blest. Amen.

One Thing Needful

"MARTHA, MARTHA, YOU ARE ANXIOUS AND TROUBLED ABOUT MANY THINGS; ONE THING IS NEEDFUL. MARY HAS CHOSEN THE GOOD PORTION, WHICH SHALL NOT BE TAKEN AWAY FROM HER." *Luke 10:41-42*

The evangelist understood very well the principle of artistic contrast. Chronologically this little scene at Bethany belongs after the visit of Jesus to the house of Zacchaeus, but the Gospel puts it before—beside the larger canvas of the parable of the Good Samaritan. "To do the will of Jesus, this is best," and that means to be active, like the Samaritan trudging the road from Jerusalem to Jericho. But the activity of a good and helpful neighbor must be linked to the quietness of a Mary sitting at Jesus' feet in rapt attention and reflection.

Observers have recently sensed a new awareness of the need for Bible study and meditation, so Mary will be in the ascendancy for a while. Then faith can rise up again and be translated into meaningful action.

In his autobiography, Phillips Brooks tells how he enrolled as a student at Andover Seminary to prepare himself for the ministry. He was invited to a prayer meeting and was abashed to hear the eloquent and fervent prayers with which his fellow students besought the Eternal. He could never pray like that. He could never put his inarticulate longings into such fervent outpourings. What spiritual giants these men must be. But what was his amazement the next morning to hear these fervent souls report "unprepared" in recitation hall! He made this devasting comment in his diary: "Their boiler had no connection with the engine."

What we need and what the world needs is the ears and heart of Mary, and the hands and zeal of Martha.

> Spread, O spread, thou mighty word,
> Spread the kingdom of the Lord,
> That to earth's remotest bound
> Men may heed the joyful sound. Amen.

Face to Face

AND WHEN THE HOUR CAME, JESUS SAT AT TABLE, AND THE APOSTLES WITH HIM. *Luke 22:14*

It is beyond comprehension that the disciples were so oblivious of the brewing storm that was soon to break over their defenseless heads, but for the moment at least they were sobered and calmed by the words and presence of Jesus himself. For us that word and presence is given in a special way at the Lord's table.

Perhaps we can approach the meaning of the Lord's Supper by meditating upon the lines of a familiar hymn, whose first line runs, "Here, O my Lord, I see thee face to face." When we come to the Lord's table, the years fade away, the miles no longer divide, for he is with us still. Robert Browning expresses the mystery of Christ's living presence:

> That one Face, far from vanish, rather grows,
> Or decomposes but to recompose,
> Become my universe that feels and knows!

Yes, I see him here.

Again, "Here, would I touch and handle things unseen."

The unleavened bread they had already eaten was the bread of God's sustaining gift in the old covenant. The blood of the Passover lamb once slain had brought them life and redemption in Egypt. *This* bread they now eat, Jesus says, is his body, his very self. He is the bread of life. *This* cup of wine they now drink points to the lifeblood to be shed on the cross, the new and living sacrifice. The "things unseen" that I here "touch and handle" are "love deep as heaven offered to men, over and over and over again."

Finally, "Here grasp with firmer hand the eternal grace, and all my weariness upon thee lean." The gift is my strength and sustenance. His word is my assurance: "Given for you." Thanks be to God!

> *This is the hour of banquet and of song;*
> *This is the heavenly table spread for me;*
> *Here let me feast, and, feasting, still prolong*
> *The brief bright hour of fellowship with thee. Amen.*

With You

AND JESUS SAID TO THEM, "I HAVE EARNESTLY DESIRED TO EAT THIS PASSOVER WITH YOU BEFORE I SUFFER; FOR I TELL YOU I SHALL NEVER EAT IT AGAIN UNTIL IT IS FULFILLED IN THE KINGDOM OF GOD. *Luke 22:15*

For the church altar at Wittenberg, Lucas Cranach painted a picture of the Last Supper. The strange thing about it is that you see not twelve but thirteen disciples, and the thirteenth was his friend Martin Luther! Purists quibble over the anachronism, but there is precious truth here.

There sits Peter. He is so sure of himself because "pride goes before destruction." He needs the promise of the sacrament that though his sins be or become as scarlet, they shall be made white as snow.

Judas sits there too. According to Luke's Gospel even the

betrayer was not excluded from participation. When remorse for his perfidy flooded his soul, grace would have brought him renewal—if he had only remembered.

There sit all the rest of the disciples too. How soon they would take to their heels and flee. How quickly they would fall asleep in the garden—and in the world, where vigilance is the price of survival. "I steadier step when I recall, that though I slip, thou dost not fall."

And that's why I find courage to come too. "Take and eat," says Jesus. "It's for sinners."

Grant, O Lord, that the ears which have heard the voice of thy songs may be closed to the voice of clamor and dispute; that the eyes which have seen thy great love may also behold thy blessed hope; that the tongues which have sung thy praise may speak the truth; that the feet which have walked in thy courts may walk in the region of light; and that the souls of all who have received thy blessed Sacrament may be restored to newness of life. Glory be to thee for thy unspeakable gift. Amen.

As One Who Serves

A DISPUTE ALSO AROSE AMONG THEM, WHICH OF THEM WAS TO BE REGARDED AS THE GREATEST. AND JESUS SAID TO THEM, "THE KINGS OF THE GENTILES EXERCISE LORDSHIP OVER THEM; AND THOSE IN AUTHORITY OVER THEM ARE CALLED BENEFACTORS. BUT NOT SO WITH YOU; RATHER LET THE GREATEST AMONG YOU BECOME AS THE YOUNGEST, AND THE LEADER AS ONE WHO SERVES. FOR WHICH IS THE GREATER, ONE WHO SITS AT TABLE, OR ONE WHO SERVES? IS IT NOT THE ONE WHO SITS AT TABLE? BUT I AM AMONG YOU AS ONE WHO SERVES." *Luke 22:24–27*

Jesus must have been heavy of heart when he discovered what retarded pupils he had, how little impression his teaching had made. Time was now of the essence, because he would soon be taken away from his disciples in death. He asks them to choose one or the other paradigm of greatness.

The first is the pattern of secular power. "The kings of the Gentiles exercise lordship," and he adds ironically that they are called "benefactors." But power corrupts—always has and always will. The poet found one day in the desert a forlorn pedestal that once belonged to the statue of a mighty monarch. "My name is Ozymandias, King of Kings" it read; "Look on my works, ye mighty, and despair!" The poet added a fitting epitaph to this boast of power—"Nothing beside remains." "O where are kings and empires now?"

Jesus instructs his disciples that secular power is not to be their pattern: "Let the greatest among you become as the youngest, and the leader as one who serves."

The czar gave a dinner once and invited many, but only those were allowed to sit at table whose hands showed the marks of toil; the rest were bidden to wait on table. Service lasts. The promise is that those who serve will sit on thrones judging the twelve tribes of Israel. Jesus says to us: "Show me your hands" too.

> Take my hands, and let them move
> At the impulse of thy love . . .
> Take myself, and I will be
> Ever, only all for thee. Amen.

Dark Gethsemane

AND JESUS CAME OUT, AND WENT, AS WAS HIS CUSTOM, TO THE MOUNT OF OLIVES; AND THE DISCIPLES FOLLOWED HIM. AND WHEN HE CAME TO THE PLACE HE SAID TO THEM, "PRAY THAT YOU MAY NOT ENTER INTO TEMPTATION." AND HE WITHDREW FROM THEM ABOUT A STONE'S THROW, AND KNELT DOWN AND PRAYED, "'FATHER, IF THOU ART WILLING, REMOVE THIS CUP FROM ME; NEVERTHELESS NOT MY WILL, BUT THINE, BE DONE." *Luke 22:39–42*

A modern artist said, "To draw is to subtract." The good picture is the one where the artist has omitted what distracts and focuses on essentials. Luke's picture of Gethsemane is marked by significant omissions, as a glance at the Matthew and Mark accounts will show.

To be sure, Luke adds as well as subtracts. Luke alone tells of the comforting angel sent to strengthen Jesus for his ordeal. Luke alone reports the confused question of the disciples, "Shall we strike?" and subsequently, the healing touch of Christ. Most of all, Luke alone reports the words of Jesus addressed to those who "had come out against him," words that characterize this night's deeds: "This is your hour, and the power of darkness."

What then emerges? We see Jesus as the man of prayer. In the book of Hebrews our Lord is described in these profound words: "In the days of his flesh, Jesus offered up prayers and supplications, with loud cries and tears, to him who was able to save him from death, and he was heard for his godly fear. Although he was a Son, he learned obedience through what he suffered, and being made perfect he became the source of eternal salvation to all who obey him."

Still a young man, life was as dear to Jesus as it is to any of us. He did not want to die. Pain was as excruciating to him as to any of us. He did not morbidly embrace it with stoic anticipation. Yet when he knew "the price of pardon was his blood, his pity ne'er withdrew." When the cup of God's wrath upon sin was put to his lips, he drank it to the dregs. "He hath given me joy by his sorrow, and life by his death."

> Look, Father, look on his anointed face,
>   And only look on us as found in him;
> Look not on our misusings of thy grace,
>   Our prayer so languid, and our faith so dim:
> For lo, between our sins and their reward
>   We set the passion of thy Son our Lord.   Amen.

The Hour of Trial

THEN THEY SEIZED JESUS AND LED HIM AWAY, BRINGING
HIM INTO THE HIGH PRIEST'S HOUSE. PETER FOLLOWED AT
A DISTANCE; AND WHEN THEY HAD KINDLED A FIRE IN THE
MIDDLE OF THE COURTYARD AND SAT DOWN TOGETHER,
PETER SAT AMONG THEM. THEN A MAID, SEEING HIM AS HE
SAT IN THE LIGHT AND GAZING AT HIM, SAID, "THIS MAN
ALSO WAS WITH HIM." BUT HE DENIED IT, SAYING, "WOMAN,
I DO NOT KNOW HIM." AND A LITTLE LATER SOME ONE
ELSE SAW HIM AND SAID, "YOU ALSO ARE ONE OF THEM."
BUT PETER SAID, "MAN, I AM NOT." AND AFTER AN INTERVAL
OF ABOUT AN HOUR STILL ANOTHER INSISTED, SAYING, "CER-
TAINLY THIS MAN ALSO WAS WITH HIM; FOR HE IS A GALI-
LEAN." BUT PETER SAID, "MAN, I DO NOT KNOW WHAT YOU
ARE SAYING." AND IMMEDIATELY, WHILE HE WAS STILL
SPEAKING, THE COCK CROWED. AND THE LORD TURNED AND
LOOKED AT PETER. AND PETER REMEMBERED THE WORD OF
THE LORD, HOW HE HAD SAID TO HIM, "BEFORE THE COCK
CROWS TODAY, YOU WILL DENY ME THREE TIMES." AND HE
WENT OUT, AND WEPT BITTERLY.   *Luke 22:54–62*

The evangelist is not only an artist but also a dramatist.
Aristotle said that the purpose of drama was "through pity
and fear to effect the proper purgation of the emotions."

Two trials are going on simultaneously at the high priest's
house. One is held by the light of the campfire, informally,
a Court of Common Pleas as it were. The other happens to
be the Supreme Court of the land, meeting in emergency
session to try a case involving a capital offense or charge.

In the lower court the accused bears false witness, under
oath, three times over. Peter protests his ignorance of the
other man on trial inside. Like a trapped animal he twists
and squirms but cannot worm his way out of trouble.

Before the high court the other accused testifies under
oath, "From now on the Son of man shall be seated at the
right hand of power." When they question him further he
replies, "You say that I am the Son of God," signifying

that there was a semantic problem, for the same words also had a different frame of reference.

And what does it all add up to? Just this: "faithless church —faithful Lord." The church of which Peter is now the sole representative, since the other disciples have fled, tries to make it up with the world, snuggling up awkwardly to the fire, pretending to be what it is not.

Nothing can save such a church except that which also rescued Peter, as a brand from the burning—the look of Christ. The eyes of Christ are not only on the weak and vacillating denier but also on the powerful and fearless apostle, the Rock, the church that was to be! At his look Peter turns away from his muted witness and the tears begin to flow, tears brought forth by a caring Spirit that broods over a beloved creature as at the creation of the world. Tears like that derive not from the worldly grief that produces death, as in Judas, but from the godly grief that means repentance unto life and salvation.

> *In the hour of trial, Jesus, plead for me,*
> *Lest by base denial I depart from thee;*
> *When thou seest me waver, with a look recall,*
> *Nor from fear or favor suffer me to fall. Amen.*

THE PASCHAL LAMB

To the Judgment Hall

PILATE ADDRESSED THEM ONCE MORE, DESIRING TO RELEASE JESUS; BUT THEY SHOUTED OUT, "CRUCIFY, CRUCIFY HIM!" A THIRD TIME HE SAID TO THEM, "WHY, WHAT EVIL HAS HE DONE? I HAVE FOUND IN HIM NO CRIME DESERVING DEATH; I WILL THEREFORE CHASTISE HIM AND RELEASE HIM." BUT THEY WERE URGENT, DEMANDING WITH LOUD CRIES THAT HE SHOULD BE CRUCIFIED. AND THEIR VOICES PREVAILED. SO PILATE GAVE SENTENCE THAT THEIR DEMAND SHOULD BE GRANTED. HE RELEASED THE MAN WHO HAD BEEN THROWN INTO PRISON FOR INSURRECTION AND MURDER, WHOM THEY ASKED FOR; BUT JESUS HE DELIVERED UP TO THEIR WILL.

Luke 23:20–25

Carved in the enduring granite of the Cuyahoga Court House in Cleveland is the proud motto, "Obedience to law is liberty." When a researcher probed the background of the text he found that the stonecarver had omitted one word from the original statement by Richard Hooker, a sixteenth-century churchman. It should have read, "Obedience to *divine* law is liberty." That misquotation is the nub of our modern problem. Divine sanction has been dropped from such sacred matters as truth, law, and liberty.

That was the problem Pilate faced. One look at the prisoner before him convinced the procurator that Jesus was by no means the subversive, dangerous revolutionary he was accused of being. Once Pilate had convinced himself of the true state of affairs, there should have been no legal or political equivocation, no shameful attempt to pass the buck to Herod, a man without conscience or character. When Pilate testified, "I find no crime in this man," that should have brought about immediate dismissal of the charges, and the prisoner's release.

What a ghastly game of musical chairs the authorities played that black Friday. The religious leaders had wanted Jesus eliminated for the sake of expediency. "The whole company arose and brought him to Pilate." The game went on and on until "the voice of the people prevailed" and Jesus was sent to the cross.

The game has not yet ended. Nathan Soederblom, the great twentieth-century church leader, said it well: "Men of various classes, the guardians of religion and of public morale and of the order of society itself, united to crucify Jesus. They were men like you and me. . . . None of us can exonerate himself from a share of responsibility for what was then done. We had a share in bringing the Saviour to the Cross. The Cross accuses us all."

O Lord, sanctify us through thy truth; thy word is truth. Amen.

Cross-Bearing

AND AS THEY LED HIM AWAY, THEY SEIZED ONE SIMON OF CYRENE, WHO WAS COMING IN FROM THE COUNTRY, AND LAID ON HIM THE CROSS, TO CARRY IT BEHIND JESUS.

Luke 23:26

Simon of Cyrene is little more than a blip on the radar screen of biblical consciousness. He appears for just a moment, and then is gone, but not forgotten. No doubt he was going about his own business that gray morning and got into the traffic jam as it moved slowly to the place of execution. He winced as he saw Jesus stagger beneath the heavy crossbar, and perhaps his eyes met the glance of Jesus as Peter's had the night before. The jeering and violent mob, hungry for the most extreme form of human cruelty known, made Simon think of resigning from the human race.

"Don't get involved!" "It's none of your business!" "What can one man do?" Thus spoke prudence. But suddenly Simon found himself in the eye of the storm. A burly soldier grabbed him by the arm and shouted, "If you don't like it, smarty, suppose you carry his cross yourself." That was how it happened. One moment Simon was a spectator, the next a participant.

Cross-bearing is galling whichever way you look at it, and humiliating too. But if you carry the cross of Jesus that makes a difference. That's the way suffering becomes redemptive. Simon of Cyrene was only the first, and a host of people ever since have followed in his train.

A controversial play *The Deputy* discusses the part the Vatican played—whether it "played safe"—in the persecution of the Jews by the Nazis. It implies that the pope thought Rome too was "worth a mass," and that he sought to save the holy city at the cost of speaking softly to the Nazis. But there can be no question at all about the everlasting rightness of the priest in the play who bravely put on his own arm the yellow band, and the Star of David, to die as a martyr for and with Christ's own brothers and sisters.

> *Jesus, I my cross have taken,*
>   *All to leave and follow thee;*
> *Destitute, despised, forsaken,*
>   *Thou from hence my all shalt be.   Amen.*

Forgiveness

AND WHEN THEY CAME TO THE PLACE WHICH IS CALLED THE SKULL, THERE THEY CRUCIFIED HIM, AND THE CRIMINALS, ONE ON THE RIGHT AND ONE ON THE LEFT. AND JESUS SAID, "FATHER, FORGIVE THEM; FOR THEY KNOW NOT WHAT THEY DO."   *Luke 23:33–34*

With characteristic vigor, Martin Luther, considering the

cruelty of man to the Son of man, said, "If I were God, and the world had treated me as it treated him, I'd kick the wretched thing to bits." Violence begets violence, as we see on TV and on the streets almost every day. The ancients told of the god-man Prometheus who was chained to the rock and tortured for three thousand years by vultures. His response was to curse the gods. Had he been able to do so Prometheus too would have kicked the universe to bits. But here at the place called The Skull we hear the opposite. Jesus pleads with God to "forgive them for they know not what they do."

That is the human story from the days of Adam to the present moment. Of every age and group it can be said: "They did not know what they were doing."

But there is the even greater mystery of forgiveness. John Donne speaks of it in the words of our prayer.

> *Wilt thou forgive that sin where I begun,*
>   *Which is my sin, though it were done before?*
> *Wilt thou forgive that sin, through which I run,*
>   *And do run still: though still I do deplore?*
>   *When thou hast done, thou hast not done,*
>   *For I have more.*
>
> *Wilt thou forgive that sin by which I have won*
>   *Others to sin? and made my sin their door?*
> *Wilt thou forgive that sin which I did shun*
>   *A year or two, but wallowed in, a score?*
>   *When thou hast done, thou hast not done,*
>   *For I have more.*
>
> *I have a sin of fear, that when I have spun*
>   *My last thread, I shall perish on the shore;*
> *Swear by thyself that at my death thy son*
>   *Shall shine, as he shines now, and heretofore;*
>   *And, having done that, thou hast done,*
>   *I fear no more.*   *Amen.*

Today in Paradise

"JESUS, REMEMBER ME WHEN YOU COME IN YOUR KINGLY POWER." AND JESUS SAID TO HIM, "TRULY, I SAY TO YOU, TODAY YOU WILL BE WITH ME IN PARADISE."   *Luke 23:42–43*

A large sign at the brow of a scarcely perceived rise in Minnesota proclaims the traveler to be standing on the North/South continental divide. From here drops of rain on one side of an unmarked line find their way at last to the frozen North Atlantic, while other drops only inches removed make their way into the Gulf of Mexico.

People too know a parting of the ways. The hill of Golgotha marked a divide for the two men who hung dying on crosses to the right and left of our Lord's cross.

One man alternated between a prayer for help and foul imprecations. Apparently he did not hear Jesus' word, "Father, forgive them." He railed at Jesus, demanding aid.

How different the other. Dismas knows he has deserved this fate. He seems also to believe that Jesus did not. He may even have indulged in a bit of gallows humor in turning to Jesus with that last request: "Don't forget the chap who walked the last mile with you to your coronation!"

What an answer he got! "Today"—from this very moment; "with me"—no longer alone in the valley of the shadow; "in Paradise"—not in death's dark vale but in the king's garden, Paradise restored by the obedience of the second Adam. For most of us it is that word which has made the difference, and divided the spirits, ever since. Copernicus of Prague voices its saving significance in the words of our prayer:

Not the favor thou gavest to a Paul, nor the grace thou didst bestow upon Peter, but only the loving-kindness thou didst show the malefactor on the cross—that, earnestly, do I desire. Amen.

Into Thy Hands

IT WAS NOW ABOUT THE SIXTH HOUR, AND THERE WAS
DARKNESS OVER THE WHOLE LAND UNTIL THE NINTH HOUR,
WHILE THE SUN'S LIGHT FAILED; AND THE CURTAIN OF THE
TEMPLE WAS TORN IN TWO. THEN JESUS, CRYING WITH A
LOUD VOICE, SAID, "FATHER, INTO THY HANDS I COMMIT MY
SPIRIT!" AND HAVING SAID THIS HE BREATHED HIS LAST.

Luke 23:44–46

The last word from the cross sums up the mission of
Jesus and the meaning of the cross. It is a prayer for peace.
Simply and lovingly we repeat the words one by one.

It begins with the word "Father." A great New Testament scholar who was asked which of the words of Jesus
undeniably fell from the Lord's lips answered without hesi-
tation, "Abba, Father." The word was on Jesus' lips that
day in the temple when to his mother's pained inquiry he
responded: "How is it that you sought me? Did you not
know that I must be in my Father's house?" When Jesus
taught his disciples, he urged upon them, "Your Father
knows. He cares for you." In Jesus' story of the prodigal son
it is the waiting Father who comes running to meet his returning, repentant children. Finally, when death drew near
and Jesus was praying in the garden, it was again the familiar
word that sprang to his lips: "Father, if thou art willing . . .
nevertheless, not my will, but thine, be done."

A young Roman father in Van Dyke's story "The Lost
Name" barters the name by which he had invoked God for
the poor prizes this world gives or sells at the devil's booth.
He could now no longer pray for help or guidance, no
longer lift holy and grateful hands of prayer, for how can
you call upon God if you know not the name by which he
is entreated? At last he heard the crucial word when his
injured boy, returning to consciousness, whimpered the name

that is above every other name, the name "Father." Jesus never lost that name, even in death.

In ancient Israel children were taught by their mothers to pray a little evening prayer, the words of Psalm 31, "Into thy hand I commit my spirit." With these words the child Jesus for years had fallen asleep in his room above the carpenter shop in Nazareth. With no pillow beneath his head, the man from Nazareth now falls asleep at the end of his life's day. Son of Mary, Son of God, he prayed the same pillow prayer.

Because he lived and died in this faith, we too can pray at all times, "I fear no foe with thee at hand to bless"; we too are confident now that "ills have no weight and tears no bitterness"; as we enter into the valley of the shadow we too can ask, "Where is death's sting, where grave thy victory?" We too are more than conquerors for now we can cry in life and in death, "I triumph still if thou abide with me."

With the whole Christian church we pray: Almighty God, we beseech thee graciously to behold this thy family, for which our Lord Jesus Christ was contented to be betrayed and given up into the hands of wicked men, and to suffer death upon the cross. Amen.

A Death So Noble

NOW THERE WAS A MAN NAMED JOSEPH FROM THE JEWISH TOWN OF ARIMATHEA. HE WAS A MEMBER OF THE COUNCIL, A GOOD AND RIGHTEOUS MAN, WHO HAD NOT CONSENTED TO THEIR PURPOSE AND DEED, AND HE WAS LOOKING FOR THE KINGDOM OF GOD. THIS MAN WENT TO PILATE AND ASKED FOR THE BODY OF JESUS. THEN HE TOOK IT DOWN AND WRAPPED IT IN A LINEN SHROUD, AND LAID HIM IN A ROCK-HEWN TOMB, WHERE NO ONE HAD EVER YET BEEN LAID. IT WAS THE DAY OF PREPARATION, AND THE SABBATH WAS BEGINNING. THE WOMEN WHO HAD COME WITH HIM FROM

GALILEE FOLLOWED, AND SAW THE TOMB, AND HOW HIS BODY WAS LAID; THEN THEY RETURNED, AND PREPARED SPICES AND OINTMENTS. ON THE SABBATH THEY RESTED ACCORDING TO THE COMMANDMENT. *Luke 23:50–56*

Setting to music the immortal story of the Passion of our Lord, Johann Sebastian Bach closes his masterpiece with a deeply devotional chorale marked by the rhythms of a lullaby, the voice of mother church crooning over Jesus' rock-hewn cradle, joined by choirs of angels singing our Savior to his night's repose. A holy sabbath hush broods over the voice of the Evangelist telling of the deposition from the cross and the burial in the tomb. But no other word is spoken. No soldier's cry, no shout from the mob, no priests, scoffers, or blasphemers disturb the silence of this final hour.

Milton, remembering the death of Samson said, "Here is nothing for tears, nothing to wail or knock the breast; no weakness, no contempt, dispraise, or blame; nothing but well and fair, and what may quiet us in a death so noble." Could he say more at the death of God's holy one? He has gone where "the wicked cease from troubling and the weary be at rest."

So Joseph of Arimathea performs the last loving rites for One he had admired from afar. Joseph is called "a good and righteous man." His goodness was shown first by this: hopelessly outnumbered in the council that had decided Jesus must be put to death, "he had not consented to their purpose and deed."

We still need such people, leaders like the latter-day president who, outnumbered and defeated, could say, "I would rather be defeated in a cause that will one day triumph, than triumph in a cause that will one day be defeated." Joseph, daring to believe that the voice of the people is not necessarily the voice of God, listened for the voice of eternity.

Joseph, moreover, was "looking for the kingdom of God."

He was one of those who believed that truth crucified will rise again. He believed that "behind the dim unknown, standeth God within the shadows keeping watch above his own." How could he know that the kingdom, and the power, and the glory was only three days away?

Finally, this good and righteous man defiled himself religiously, doing what he had to do. By touching a corpse he disqualified himself from keeping the Passover. A person that good and righteous is hard to find!

With Joseph and all who watch beside the sepulcher we pray:

> Here yet awhile, Lord, thou art sleeping,
>   Hearts turn to thee, O Saviour blest:
>   Rest thou calmly, calmly rest.
> Death that holds thee in its keeping,
>   When its bonds are loosed by thee,
> Shall become a welcome portal,
> Leading to the life immortal,
>   Where he shall thy glory see.
>   Saviour blest,
>   Slumber now, and take thy rest.   Amen.

THE TABLE AT EMMAUS

The Glory Road

SO THEY DREW NEAR TO THE VILLAGE TO WHICH THEY WERE GOING. JESUS APPEARED TO BE GOING FURTHER, BUT THEY CONSTRAINED HIM, SAYING, "STAY WITH US, FOR IT IS TOWARD EVENING AND THE DAY IS NOW FAR SPENT." SO HE WENT IN TO STAY WITH THEM. WHEN HE WAS AT TABLE WITH THEM, HE TOOK THE BREAD AND BLESSED, AND BROKE IT, AND GAVE IT TO THEM. AND THEIR EYES WERE OPENED AND THEY RECOGNIZED HIM; AND HE VANISHED OUT OF THEIR SIGHT. THEY SAID TO EACH OTHER, "DID NOT OUR HEARTS BURN WITHIN US WHILE HE TALKED TO US ON THE ROAD, WHILE HE OPENED TO US THE SCRIPTURES?" AND THEY ROSE THAT SAME HOUR AND RETURNED TO JERUSALEM; AND THEY FOUND THE ELEVEN GATHERED TOGETHER AND THOSE WHO WERE WITH THEM, WHO SAID, "THE LORD HAS RISEN INDEED, AND HAS APPEARED TO SIMON!" THEN THEY TOLD WHAT HAD HAPPENED ON THE ROAD, AND HOW HE WAS KNOWN TO THEM IN THE BREAKING OF THE BREAD.

Luke 24:28–35

The Evangelist divides that first Easter Day into three parts. He recounts the events of the morning, afternoon, and evening.

Luke offers no description of the resurrection. Life from the tomb, as life from the womb, is God's own secret; it is not for probing, human eyes to behold. But the fact of the resurrection is proclaimed! By the time the sun rises, the Son has already risen. To the startled, incredulous, and fearful women arriving at the tomb by "early dawn," the angels speak only what must have seemed to ordinary mortals an idle tale, "Why do you seek the living among the dead?" How can these things be? "Ashes to ashes, dust to dust, as of the unjust, so of the just; yea of that Just One too, this is the one sad gospel that is true, 'Christ is not risen!' " So speaks man's unbelieving heart always.

On Easter afternoon two disciples turn their faces toward home. Talking as they walk, they discourse upon the rumors that had begun to circulate, but founder on the rock that still lay, for all they knew, on the fast-closed tomb. A stranger joins them. He talks of the divine necessity of the Savior's suffering, and of how all the prophets had foretold the things that had come to pass that past week in Jerusalem. "And beginning with Moses and all the prophets, he interpreted to them in all the scriptures the things concerning himself." What had seemed to the eleven merely an "idle tale" now began to make sense. Faith glimmered as their hearts were strangely warmed, and they began to feed their souls at the Table of the Word.

Then at nightfall, as the day was far spent, they invited their newfound friend to sit at the table they were preparing for him. But as he sat, it was he that took the bread as host, not guest, and breaking it lifted up his eyes to heaven and gave thanks. Then their eyes were opened and they knew him, their living, loving Lord. They knew now that he could not be "holden of death," that he was alive for evermore. In the fellowship of the Jerusalem disciples they heard the words that the church has repeated wonderingly and triumphantly ever since: "The Lord is risen. He is risen indeed. Hallelujah!"

Where Christ met them that first Easter, he meets us still. Where two or three are gathered together to search for the Word of God, he is there in our midst. Whether few or many, whether two or two hundred or three thousand souls as on the day of Pentecost, he draws near and our hearts are still warmed when his word is proclaimed. So too, when his bread is broken, when he prepares a table before us in the sacrament, we not only show forth his death until he comes, but he himself draws near in living presence.

> *Be known to us in breaking bread,*
> *But do not then depart;*
> *Saviour, abide with us, and spread*
> *Thy table in our heart. Amen.*